Copyright Notice ....

Potted History ....

The Walks ....

Get Ready ....

The Maps 7

Walk 1 - Lower Town 8

Walk 2 - Cathedral and Castle 31

Walk 3 - Along the River 75

Did you Enjoy these Walks? 98

Other Strolling Around Books to Try 99

Index 100

Copyright Notice

Strolling Around Durham by Irene Reid

ISBN: 9798301370915

All rights reserved. This book may not be reproduced in any form, in whole or in part, without written permission from the author.

The author has made every effort to ensure the accuracy of the information in this book at the time of going to press and cannot accept responsibility for any consequences arising from the use of the book.

Book Cover
Photo Sanctuary Ring by Irene Reid

Enhanced by Prisma Photo Editor

Potted History

People have lived in this area since 2000 BCE, but Durham's history really starts with the story of Saint Cuthbert.

Saint Cuthbert

Saint Cuthbert was a monk who lived in various monasteries in his lifetime, but most famously on the Isle of Lindisfarne, where he became bishop and died in 687.

Eleven years after his death the monks decided to open his coffin up and they discovered that his body had not decomposed at all. So not surprisingly, Cuthbert was declared a saint.

Since the Isle of Lindisfarne sits undefended in the North Sea, it was often raided by the Vikings. So eventually the monks took the decision to flee the island with all their holy relics – including Saint Cuthbert.

They wandered around the North of England for years – always avoiding the Vikings. One day they arrived near present day Durham.

At this point, legend takes over. The cart carrying the coffin of Saint Cuthbert stopped and could not be moved. Bishop Aldhum, who was leading the monks, suddenly had a vision - Saint Cuthbert instructed the bishop that he should be taken to Dunholme. The problem was, none of the monks knew where that might be.

Just then a farm maid arrived looking for a cow which she had lost at "Dun Holm". The monks put two and two together and decided to follow the farm maid to Dun Holm. The monks tried to push the cart again, and miraculously it moved, letting them follow the farm maid.

Dunholme is of course modern-day Durham, and where the monks built their first wooden church. They later replaced it with a stone church called the White Church.

The Normans

After the Norman Conquest in 1066, Dunholme was identified as highly defensible since it sits high on a hill and is surrounded on three sides by the River Wear. So, a mighty castle was built by William the Conqueror, and Dunholme became an important defence point against the Scottish army and any local insurrections.

By the end of the eleventh century, Saint Cuthbert was drawing pilgrims like a magnet. So, like all good churches the monks decided to build bigger and better, and eventually the Cathedral we have today was constructed, safely behind the castle defenses.

The city of Durham grew up around the castle defences and spread down the hill towards the river.

Coal and Miners

During the industrial revolution coal was mined extensively around Durham, and today the miners and their associations still play a large part in the traditions and culture of Durham.

Although the mining industry is a shadow of its former self, the annual "Big Meeting" (the Durham Miners Gala) still takes place in July every year.

The highlight is the parade of banners accompanied by a brass band. After the speeches there is a service for the miners in the cathedral, where the banners are once again on display.

The banners are all very colourful with illustrations of famous names from mining history, and slogans such as "Need before greed".

The Great Flood

In 1771 a combination of ice thawing and persistent torrential rain resulted in The Great Flood. It affected large areas of Northern England including Durham. Durham lost two bridges and its corn mill.

University

It was not until the early nineteenth century that the University as we know it today was founded.

It's the third oldest in England after Oxford and Cambridge, and just like them it consists of different colleges, 17 of them.

The University owns or uses most of the buildings in the upper town, including the castle. If it's term time you will see a lot of students as you explore the city.

The Walks

Walk 1 – This walk starts at Framwellgate Bridge. It takes you around the lower town and then up Silver Street.

Walk 2 – This walk takes you from Silver Street to the upper town and includes the castle and the cathedral.

Walk 3 – This walk takes you from the cathedral down to the riverside and then along the riverside back to Framwellgate Bridge.

As you can see, the three walks all join up to form a loop. So, with a bit of brisk walking, you could squeeze them all into one day – although you might find it difficult to fit in an in depth visit to the cathedral and the castle.

Get Ready
Decide if you want to take a tour of the cathedral and/or the castle. You can tour the cathedral independently, but you will need to join the official tour if you wish to see the inside of the castle.

Both can be purchased online before you visit to ensure a timeslot.

The Maps
There are maps sprinkled all through the walks to help you find your way. If you need to check where you are at any point during a walk, always flip back to find the map you need.

To help you follow the maps, each map shows its start point. In addition, numbered directions have been placed on each map. The numbers correspond to the directions within the walks.

Walk 1 - Lower Town

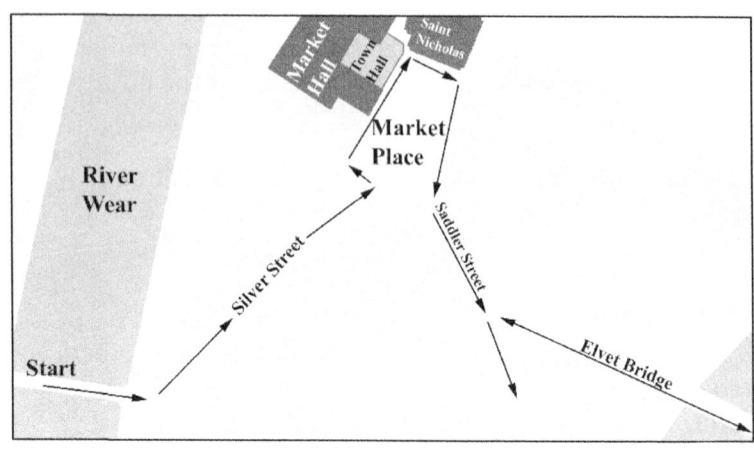

Walk 1 Overview

This walk starts on Framwellgate Bridge. It takes you first to Market Place which is the heart of the lower town. You then climb Saddler Street to approach the upper town.

Start about halfway over Framwellgate bridge.

Here you get a lovely view of both the cathedral and the castle high above you, and the river with its weir below.

Beyond the weir you can see the arches of Prebends Bridge, which you will cross over if you manage to fit Walk 3 into your explorations.

If you look in the other direction you will see the modern Millburngate Bridge and another weir.

Framwellgate Bridge

This bridge was the main entry point into Durham for centuries. Traffic now enters via the Millburngate Bridge, so Framwellgate Bridge has been pedestrianised letting you stroll over it in safety.

The first bridge to be built at this spot was erected by Bishop Flambard in the twelfth century. This one was built in the fifteenth century by Bishop Langley as a replacement, after a flood tore away the old bridge.

The existence of both bridges show how wealthy Durham was in the Middle Ages, as a stone bridge was a huge investment for any community.

It used to be guarded by both a tower and gate on the castle side of the river. They were torn down with the arrival of the car to allow traffic to use the bridge. The bridge would also once have had shops on it, but those too have long disappeared.

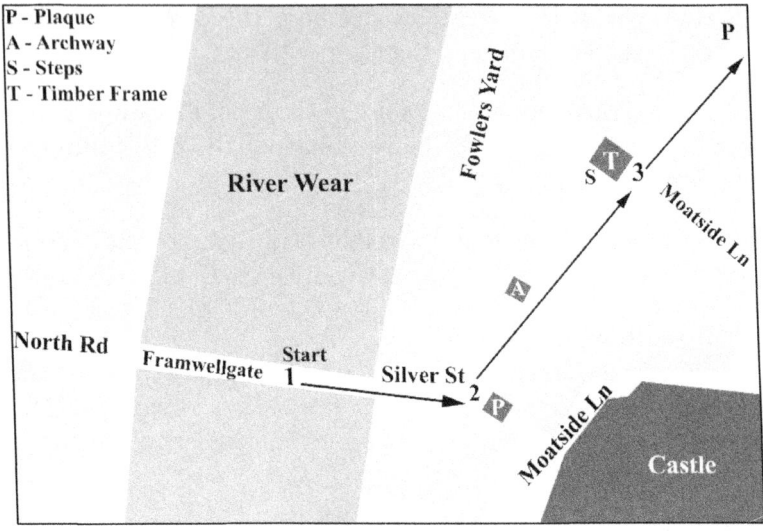

Map 1.1

Map 1.1 - With the cathedral on your right-hand side, cross the bridge into Silver Street. Pause as the street bends left.

Silver Street

It's often said that Silver Street gets its name from the bishop's mint, however the mint was actually up near the castle and well within its defensive walls. It's more likely that the street's name comes from the silversmiths who plied their trade here.

Spot the little alley with a plaque above it on the bend. It is called Moatside Lane.

Moatside Lane

For centuries, pilgrims crossed the bridge into Silver Street as you just did. They would then have walked along the side of the moat which lay outside the castle's defensive wall to reach the North Gate. They would then pass through the gate to reach the Cathedral.

Moatside Lane follows the path the pilgrims would have taken and is now a shortcut up to the cathedral. You might want to use it later, but for now you should follow Silver Street round to the left and explore the lower town.

Map 1.2 - Climb Silver Street as it bends to the left. Pause when you see a set of narrow steps on your left leading down to an archway.

The house just beyond the steps is a very old timber framed house from the seventeenth century.

Map 1.3 - Continue up the hill.

A few steps further on, you will see another narrow lane on your right which is a second way to reach Moatside Lane.

Continue up Silver Street. Pause at the top of the hill just before the street starts to widen as it meets Market Place.

On your left you can find another of Durham's commemorative plaques. It sits between two shop windows.

Sir John Duck

It marks where Sir John Duck's mansion once stood. Sadly, it has gone, and we are left with a very boring modern building.

John Duck came to Durham hoping to become a butcher's apprentice. However, no-one would employ him because he could not prove where he came from, and the butchers feared he was a Scot. Employing Scots was forbidden by the Butcher's Guild.

Legend tells us that he was down by the river, contemplating what to do next, when a passing raven dropped a gold coin at his feet.

He used that coin to start his own business and was incredibly successful. He ended up as mayor and one of the wealthiest citizens in Durham, although it's also been suggested that he wasn't averse to a bit of dishonest trading to get to the top.

He later became a baronet and took the title "Sir John Duck of Haswell on the Hill".

He died in 1691 and is buried in St Margarets Church in Durham. His mansion which stood here was torn down just last century.

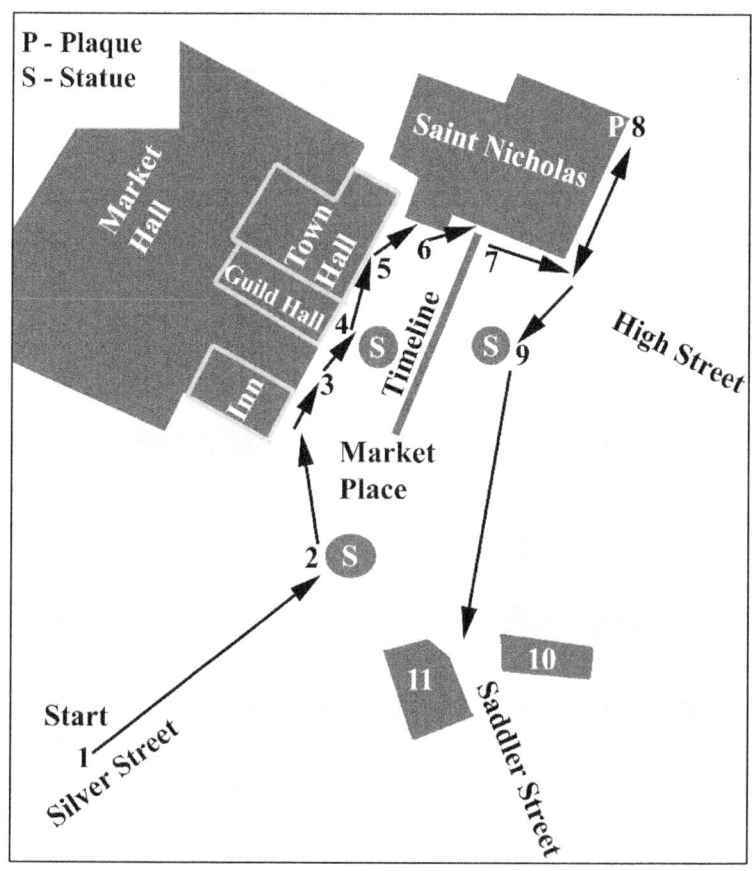

Map 2

Map 2.1 - Now enter Market Place.

Market Place

Market Place, as its name suggests, was where the market was held in the Middle Ages.

Make your way to the imposing statue of the third Marquess of Londonderry who is sitting on his horse.

Marquess of Londonderry

This statue is referred to by the locals simply as "The Horse".

The Marquess of Londonderry fought in the Napoleonic wars at the Duke of Wellington's side. He led a brigade of hussars – so here he sits on his warhorse dressed in hussar uniform.

The hussars were originally a Hungarian light cavalry from the fifteenth century, hence the rather exotic-looking uniform.

He married a local heiress and with her wealth he invested in the coal mining industry. On the good side he built the Seaham harbour, the County of Durham's only harbour. However, he was a very unpopular man.

Among many repressive and exploitive actions against the workers, he led a campaign against the Mines and Collieries Act 1842, insisting he had the right to use children in his mines.

He is quoted as stating:

"With respect to the age at which males should be admitted into mines, the members of this association have unanimously agreed to fix it at eight years... In the thin coal mines, it is more especially requisite that boys, varying in age from eight to fourteen, should be employed; as the underground roads could not be made of sufficient height for taller persons without incurring an outlay so great as to render the working of such mines unprofitable".

By the time of the Great Irish Famine, he was one of the richest men in the UK, but he gave a pittance to help the starving.

A lovely man!

When he died his wife commissioned this statue and presented it to the city. Durham didn't really want it and tried to have it placed on Palace Green up by the Cathedral instead, however the monks politely declined the offer, so here it is.

There is an odd legend about the statue. It's said that its creator, Signor Raphael Monti from Milan, was so proud of his creation that he offered a prize to anyone who could find a flaw in his perfect creation. Legend says that a blind beggar examined the statue and declared that the horse was missing its tongue, and Monti was so horrified that he killed himself. However, it's just a legend, the statue does indeed have a tongue, and Monti went on to create many more statues.

Face the same direction as the Marquess, then look to your left to spot the Market Tavern.

Market Tavern

This inn was originally called The City Tavern but was renamed in 1865.

It was here that the Durham Miners' Association came into being in 1869. The miners chose to stand together to fight for better lives, and against working conditions such as those demanded by the Marquess of Londonderry!

So, you might want to consider popping in for a pint at some point, and drink to those first unionists.

Map 2.2 - Face the same direction as the Marquess.

Walk down the left-hand side of the square to reach the entrance to the Market Hall.

Beyond the entrance you will see the Guildhall with its balcony, and finally the Town Hall – all very handsome buildings.

The Market Hall itself actually sits behind and wraps around both the Town Hall and the Guild Hall.

Map 2.3 - Make your way to stand in front of the guildhall.

Guildhall

Durham was awarded its city charter in the twelfth century. The various tradesmen in the city formed themselves into guilds, and the first guildhall was built in the fourteenth century. The trade guilds enforced strict rules on its members to protect businesses and reputations.

The guilds also enjoyed ceremonies and parades in medieval times. The parades started here in Market Place outside the guildhall, and the guildsman marched to Palace Green outside the Cathedral.

In the seventeenth century Durham's first mayor was appointed; he was elected by the senior guildmembers who were known as the aldermen.

The Guildhall is where the city keeps its links to the past, the city charter and the ceremonial sword. Durham is the only city other than London to have a bodyguard for its mayor. The pikes traditionally used by the bodyguard are also kept in the guildhall.

Unfortunately at the time of writing, the guildhall is not open to the public very often. But perhaps that will have changed when you visit.

Just outside the Guildhall stands the Durham Light Infantry statue. Walk over to it.

Durham Light Infantry statue

This statue was installed in 2014 to commemorate the men of the Durham Light Infantry. On the plinth you see the regiment's cap badge, which includes a bugle. Below that you can read:

DEDICATED TO ALL WHO SERVED IN THE REGIMENT
AND IN MEMORY OF THOSE WHO GAVE THEIR LIVES IN THE
CAUSE OF FREEDOM

It was the buglers who sounded the end of the Korean war in 1953, from a hilltop on the front line. It was the infantry's last battleground.

The regiment had a long history and won many honours; It won 38 battle honours and eleven Victoria Crosses. In WWII they fought under General Mongomery in El Alamein. He is quoted as saying:

> "There may be some Regiments as good
> but I know of none better"

The Durham Light Infantry was merged into The Rifles in 2007.

Map 2.4 – Continue to the Town Hall which is next door.

Town Hall

Both the Victorian Town Hall and the Market Hall stand on what used to be the home of the Neville family, an ancient and very important family from this part of County Durham.

If you are lucky enough to be here on a Saturday, you can pop in for a look around. It's free and is very interesting.

Great Hall

The Great Hall inside the Town Hall is well worth seeing, with its colourful stained-glass windows, coats of arms, and splendid wooden roof.

There are a number of plaques on the walls of the Great Hall. They commemorate freemen of the city, including some well-known names such as Bill Bryson and Archbishop Desmond Tutu. Freemen gain certain rights including the right to have a market stall free of charge, but it's unlikely we will see Bill Bryson selling his books in the market.

The Hallway

In the Hallway you can see a statue, and a display case holding the clothes and violin of, Josef Boruwlaski.

He was Polish and because of a genetic disorder he only grew to 3 feet 3 inches tall. However, he became a musician and travelled Europe entertaining noble families and royalty, including Marie Antoinette.

At the end of the eighteenth century, he came to Britain and liked Durham so much he retired here. He wrote a poem:

> Poland was my Cradle
> England is my nest
> Durham is my quiet place
> where my weary bones shall rest.

He is buried in the cathedral, and you can find exactly where on Walk 2.

Lantern Room

This is a simple room, but it is beautifully illuminated by a stained-glass dome which looks very Art Nouveau.

The room is home to all sorts of historic items treasured by Durham. Don't miss the colourful Durham Light Infantry banner which lists all their foreign engagements. As mentioned earlier, the list ends with the Korea War in 1953. They also served in Afghanistan, but in those days, it was spelled Affghanistan.

Map 2.5 – When you exit, walk towards the church you can see at the end of the square.

St Nicholas Church

The locals call it St Nics.

The original church which stood here was pulled down in 1857 and this is its replacement. The first church was longer and joined the city wall. It also had a small graveyard on this side of the square, but it has disappeared under the square's flagstones.

The new church was designed by a local architect in the nineteenth century. In an edition of the Illustrated London News, it was described as:

> The most beautiful specimen of church architecture
> in the north of England

The new church was made shorter so that Silver Street, which leaves the square at the end of the church, could be widened. It was given a handsome spire and beautiful windows. The spire has six bells, five of them having been saved from the old church.

Above the church door you can see Saint Nicholas himself. He is the patron saint of merchants, so he is an appropriate saint to keep an eye over the market square.

If you are lucky enough to find the church open, pop in for a look. It has been extensively restored and has some interesting touches such as the modern stained-glass windows. Spot the intriguing metal and glass fish which decorates one of the arches. The fish is an old Christian symbol.

Map 2.6 - When back outside, make your way to stand between the first two windows to the right of the church door.

Timeline

Spot the line of granite paving stones which run from the church all the way up to the Marquess of Londonderry.

They illustrate the history of Durham with engraved words and pictures, the first of course being the journey of Saint Cuthbert to Durham.

You might want to return here once you have explored Durham to have another look at them.

Map 2.7 - Walk along the church on Market Place then go round the corner into Silver Street. Walk to the far corner of the church.

Clayport Gate

Durham was, and still is to some extent, a walled city. You are now standing where part of the city wall once stood, sealing off the city from the north.

There were several huge gates at key positions giving access into the city:

Kings Gate
Owen Gate
North Gate
Flesher Gate
Clayport Gate
Water Gate

On the corner of the church, you will see a plaque which commemorates Clayport Gate.

Clayport Gate was built in the fourteenth century to give access from Claypath, the street which runs in front of the Gala Theatre which you can see across the busy road ahead of you. Claypath was the route to Sunderland.

Both Clayport Gate and the wall were demolished in the late eighteenth century.

Durham's City Wall

It's generally agreed that the wall built around the lower city was not nearly as substantial as that which surrounded the upper city. After all, the upper city was where the cathedral and castle stood, whereas only shops and houses filled the lower city, and they were not nearly as important to the powers that be.

The North Gate provided access between the upper and lower cities, and you can see where it stood on Walk 2.

Map 2.8 - Backtrack into Market Square and walk to the statue of Neptune.

Neptune's Pants

A pant is an old northern word for a drinking fountain, and there were several pants scattered around Durham before water was piped into houses.

In the early eighteenth century this statue of Neptune stood over a large stone octagonal pant in the centre of Market Square.

He was chosen to decorate the water fountain as he is the Roman god of the sea. It was part of a campaign to turn Durham into an inland port. The plan was to join the Tyne and the Wear rivers by a canal. However, it did not get any further than placing Neptune in Market Square.

A few decades later a new scheme was thought up. This time they planned to make the River Wear navigable all the way to Sunderland. However, as the size of ships kept rising, the alterations needed to the river became unsurmountable, and the plan was finally laid to rest.

There is a plaque on the statue's pedestal which marks the grand scheme.

As for Neptune, when the pant in Market Place was no longer needed, it was removed, and Neptune was dispatched to Wharton Park. He was struck by lightning in 1979 and was badly damaged. A fund-raising campaign was begun to restore the statue, and eventually he came home again to Market Place.

Map 2.9 - Continue uphill from Neptune to exit Market Place onto Saddler Street.

Saddler Street

This street was, and still is, the main route between the cathedral and Market Place.

Buildings have lined this street since before 1200, but obviously have been rebuilt and replaced many times. The street you are walking on now is actually several feet higher than the original street, so beneath your feet lie what's left of those old houses. Today Saddler Street is lined with mostly medieval and Georgian constructions.

As you enter the street from Market Place, on your right you will see the unusually curved façade of number 11.

Opposite it, at number 10, stands a narrow building. If you look up above the shop façade, you can see the original handsome style it was built in.

The wooden shop facade itself seems completely out of character, and if you walk past the shop and look back, you will see it is stamped 2013. It's always well worth looking above street level to see how buildings originally looked.

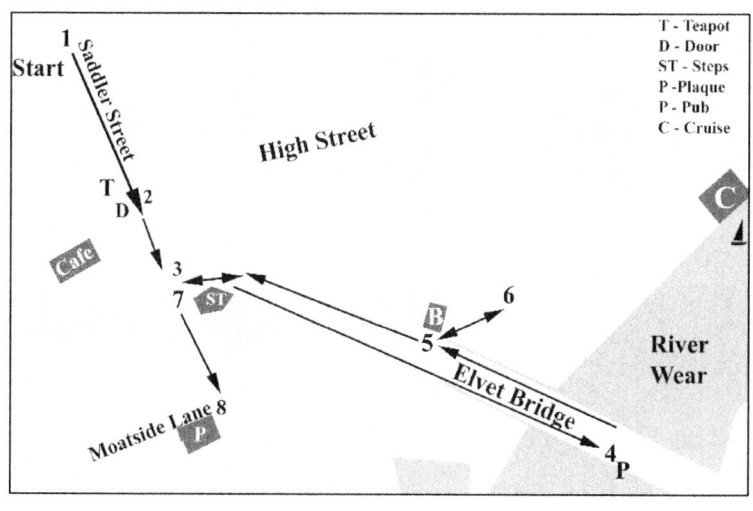

Map 3

Map 3.1 - Continue a few more steps along Saddler Street to find a golden teapot above you on your right.

The Teapot

The teapot originally appeared in 1857 and has been situated above various shops in Durham over the years.

It ended up in poor condition, so it was finally taken down and a restoration project was started. Over the years it had turned black, but it has now been restored to its golden colour and rehung here in Saddler Street.

Just next door is the Vennels Cafe building.

Durham Mustard

Durham powder was first manufactured in the Vennels Café building which lies behind this door. It was made by Mrs Clements from Durham, who devised a method of processing mustard seed into a dry mustard powder, full of strength and flavour. She got a royal patent and sold her product all over England.

As is always the case, other manufacturers soon discovered and adopted her techniques. Eventually production of mustard powder passed out of Durham and onto Colman's of Norwich.

At the time of writing there is a new mustard producer in Durham, so perhaps you might like to try it if you spot it in the shops you visit.

A few steps will bring you to High Street on your left.

High Street
Don't be fooled, High Street is really quite a modern addition to Durham. It was built to give access to the large shopping area which was built to the east of Market Place.

Map 3.2 – A few more steps up Saddler Street will bring you to a fork in the road and the Magdalene Steps.

Magdalene Steps
The steps are thought to be named after a medieval hospice which has long disappeared.

The area around the steps is currently cluttered with street signs etc. Durham should really try to tidy and enhance this lovely spot.

Map 3.3 - Descend the steps. Walk along the street called Elvet Bridge to reach Elvet Bridge itself.

Elvet Bridge
The street used to be known as Souter Peth. Souter is an old northern word for cobbler, so this was Cobbler Path. It has now adopted the name of the bridge which it gives access to.

Elvet Bridge is Durham's second oldest bridge and was built in the twelfth century. It has seven visible arches, four of which the river runs through and three which have houses built on top.

The bridge was badly damaged in the Great Flood of 1771 when its three central arches were swept away.

Make your way to the middle of the bridge where you will find a plaque on your righthand side.

The bridge was needed to give access to Elvet, which translates as Swan Island in old English. It is a settlement on the other side of the river which is thought to actually be older than the cathedral and the castle.

To help in the bridge construction, the church offered indulgences for anyone willing to help build it. An indulgence was basically a pass to commit a little sin in return for something the church wanted. Many religious buildings were built or supported this way.

The bridge used to be guarded by a tower gate, but that has long disappeared. There were also two chapels on the bridge, St Andrews, and St James, one at either end. Part of what was St Andrews is still standing above one of the bridge arches, but to see it you would need to get down to the riverside.

Map 3.4 - Backtrack to the start of the bridge. At the time of writing, on your right you will see the Tin of Sardines

Tin of Sardines

It's reputed to be the smallest gin bar in England. If its open, you might want to try to squeeze in.

Map 3.5 - Descend the steps to the right of the bar door to reach the riverside.

Jail and a Ghost

Turn to face the steps and you will see one of the bridge's dry arches . You also get a good view of the four arches which the river does flow through.

To the right of the steps, you will see an arched doorway tucked in the corner. It's the entrance to what were two prison cells which were part of the House of Correction which used to stand here.

The cells are said to be haunted by Jimmy Allan, a gypsy piper. There have also been claims of haunting pipe music being heard when crossing the Event Bridge at night.

Boat Trip

If you feel like a boat trip along the Wear, you are not far from Prince Bishop River Cruises. They have a cruiser which will take you on a one-hour trip up and down the river. It leaves on the hour. They also have rowing boats if you feel very adventurous.

If that appeals, turn round so that Elvet Bridge is behind you. Walk along the riverside passing through a narrow walkway. Once the walkway widens you will find Prince Bishop River Cruises on your right.

Return to the steps at the bottom of Elvet Bridge when you are finished cruising.

Map 3.6 - Climb back up the stairs and turn right. Walk back along the street to climb the Magdalene Steps.

Map 3.7 - Turn left along Saddler Street to reach a pub called The Shakespeare on your right. Just before it you will see two lanes. The narrowest lane which is nearest the pub is called Moatside Lane.

> Note - This is the other end of the alley which you read about on Silver Street near the start of Walk 1.
>
> It is a shortcut between Silver Street and Saddler Street which you might find useful.

Moatside Lane

Back in the eighteenth century, Durham like most sizable cities and towns, had theatres for entertainment. One of the theatres stood behind The Shakespeare and it was accessed by Moatside Lane.

The theatre was managed by a famous actor named Stephen Kemble, who is said to have played the role of Shakespeare's chubby Falstaff without the need of any padding.

The theatre was lost to a fire in 1869.

The Shakespeare

At the time of writing this pub has closed. However, it may have been re-opened when you visit. If it is, it gives you a chance to visit Durham's most haunted pub.

It was built in the twelfth century and was originally called The Ostler and Groom. It later took its current name from the actors and plays which were performed in the theatre which stood behind it.

You have now reached the end of Walk 1.

You could continue with Walk 2 which starts from this point.

Walk 2 - Cathedral and Castle

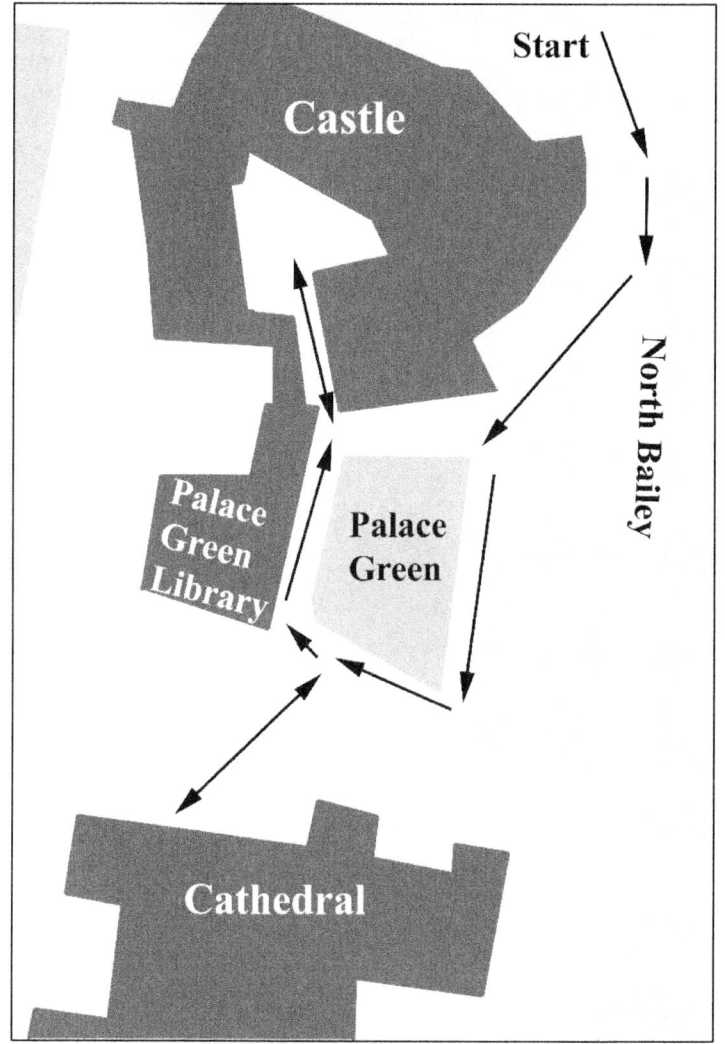

Overview Walk 2

This walk takes you from Saddler Street up to see both the Cathedral and the Castle.

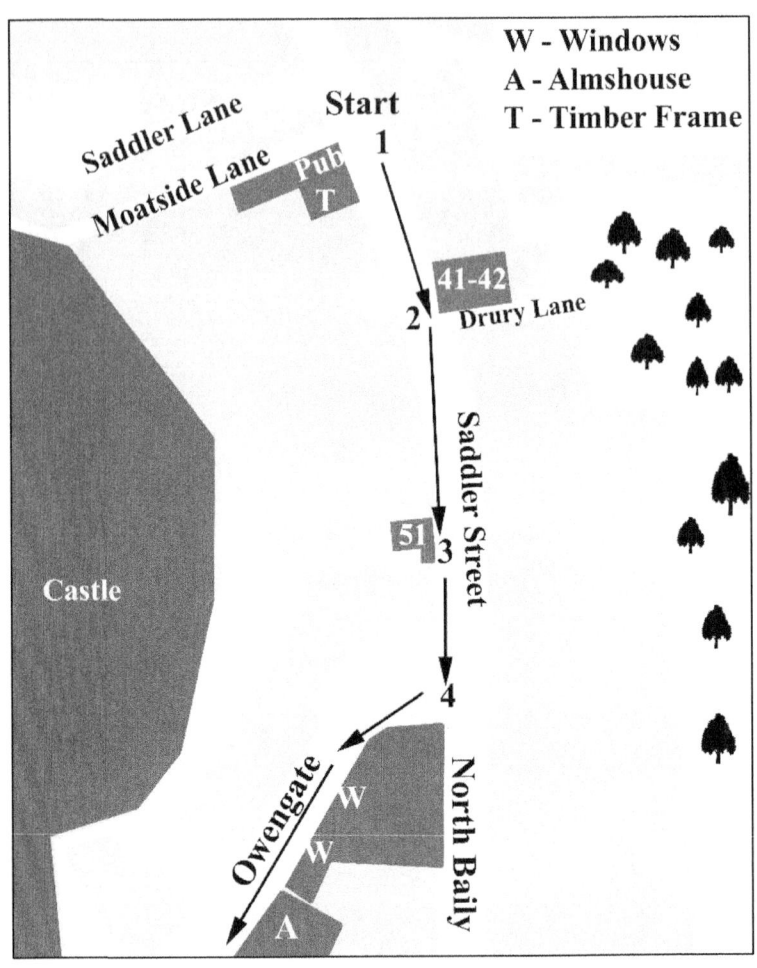

Map 1

This walk starts on Saddler Street at the entrance to Moatside Lane, just next to the Shakespeare pub.

Next to the Shakespeare pub stands a timber framed building. Unlike many in Durham, the building facade has not been rendered over and the timbers are still visible.

Map 1.1 - Face uphill and walk up Saddler Street to number 41-42 on your left.

Just beyond it, you will find an old alleyway with steps leading down. It is called Drury Lane.

Drury Lane

The alley was named after the famous London theatre district because it gave access to the city's first theatre which was built down by the riverside in the eighteenth century.

The plaque above the alley entrance commemorates its existence.

Map 1.2 - Continue along Saddler Street which now becomes a lot steeper.

As you reach number 51 on your right, you are walking over where the North Gate used to stand.

The North Gate

It guarded the castle and the cathedral from attack from the north. It was a huge construction, straddling the road and standing sixty feet high.

On your right just past number 51 you will find a rather shabby old door.

The door is usually locked but you can look through the window.

You can see a tiny piece of what is left of the North Gate which was built into the castle's defence wall. There is a plaque above the door commemorating the gate.

The North Gate later became the city jail, but it was finally demolished to allow car access up Saddler Street.

Map 1.3 - Continue up Saddler Street and you will reach a fork in the road.

The road to your right is Owengate, and the road to your left is North Bailey.

Owengate gets its name from another defensive gate which stood at the top of the street.

Map 1.4 - Walk along Owengate.

Owengate Buildings

As you walk up Owengate, take a look at the old building on your left-hand side. It is now part of the university.

It has many beautiful stone windows, and the two largest windows are decorated with little stone heads at the top corners which are very easy to miss.

Beyond the windows with the little heads is another building which used to be an almshouse. Almshouses were built to house members of a community who could not support themselves.

This one was built in the nineteenth century. It was a replacement for an older almshouse which still stands on Palace Green and which you will see soon. The university took over the older almshouse as the space was needed for expansion.

At the time of writing this building is used as a World Heritage Site Visitor Centre.

In front of you stands the Cathedral, and in front of it, Palace Green.

The cathedral's official name is Cathedral Church of Christ, Blessed Mary the Virgin, and St Cuthbert of Durham.

Palace Green

Many of England's beautiful cathedrals are let down by their modern surroundings which dimmish and even overshadow them. No better example can be found than St Pauls in London which is totally hemmed in and dwarfed by the modern buildings of London.

Durham Cathedral has been spared that. Here it stands in splendid isolation, on a hill and accompanied only by equally old and small buildings. As you approach it from one end of Palace Green you cannot but be impressed with its presence and grandeur.

Palace Green was the original marketplace and would have been filled with traders and shoppers, as well as builders working on the long construction of the cathedral. By the twelfth century the bishop had had enough of the noise and mess, and ordered that the green be cleared so that:

"The church should neither be endangered by fire nor polluted by filth".

So, the traders and shoppers shifted downhill to Market Place which you may have explored on walk 1.

However, even today, Palace Green is often filled with tents and kiosks for various events.

T - Telephone Box
P - Postbox
W - War Memorial
M - Mint

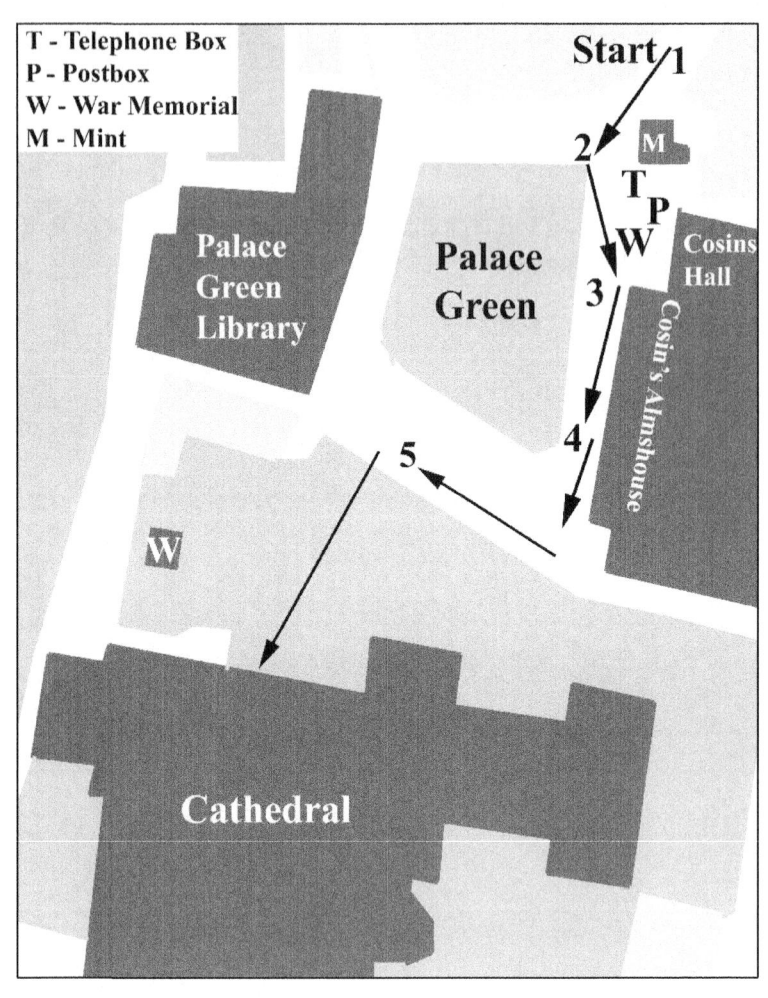

Map 2

Map 2.1 - Walk straight ahead to reach the edge of the green.

On your left you will see an old telephone box, a Victorian post box, and a Victoria Cross memorial plaque for the Durham Light Infantry,

Behind the telephone box is a building which was called Moneyer's Garth.

Moneyer's Garth

The building you see today is Victorian and is a public toilet, so it is not really that interesting.

However, it was built on top of the Prince Bishop's Mint which stood here in the twelfth century. Prince Bishops had much more power than a standard bishop, including the right to mint their own coins.

The first Prince Bishop of Durham Cathedral was Bishop Walcher, and he was appointed by William the Conqueror just after the Norman Conquest.

Bishop Walcher was given powers well beyond those of bishops in southern cathedrals. Doing so gave Wiliam the Conqueror a powerful ruler in the troublesome northern part of his new kingdom.

Later, a steward of a later bishop of Durham is quoted as saying:

"There are two kings in England, namely the Lord King of England, wearing a crown in sign of his regality and the Lord Bishop of Durham, wearing a mitre in place of a crown, in sign of his regality in the diocese of Durham."

Durham's Prince Bishops minted coins from the eleventh century to the sixteenth century. At that point King Henry VIII had the mint closed as part of his dissolution of the monasteries.

Map 2.2 – Walk to the next rather grand looking building just beyond the post-box. It is called Cosin's Hall.

Cosin's Hall

This three storeyed building was originally called the Archdeacons Inn. It is unusual in that it is a brick building. If you glance round the Green, you will see that most buildings are made of stone.

In 1833 it became University House and was where University College studied and resided. University College was the first college of Durham University.

Just a few years later University College moved into the Castle, but University House was kept to provide extra housing for students.

It was renamed after Bishop John Cosin. He was a prolific builder from the seventeenth century, and many of the constructions around the green were his ideas. However this handsome building is just named after him, he had no hand in its construction.

Map 2.3 - Continue along the green to the next long one-story building.

Cosin's Almshouse

This building was originally a school for grammar and music which was founded by Bishop Langley in the fifteenth century.

Two hundred years later Bishop Cosin turned it into an almshouse. It was then snaffled by the university and the replacement almshouse you saw on Owengate was built.

Cosin's Almshouse had 8 rooms, accommodation for 4 men and 4 women. The lucky residents had to be unmarried and deemed "honourable citizens". 6 were to come from Durham, and 2 could come from a nearby parish where Cosin had been rector.

Strict rules were in place. The residents had to attend a lot of prayers and basically avoid anything the church deemed unsavoury. However, living a sin-free life for free board and lodging was probably seen as a good deal for the poor.

Above the door you can read

> Hospitale epi Dunhelm
> Pro VIII Pauperibus
> Fundat per Joh Episcop
> AD MDCLXVI

> Episcopal Hospital of Durham
> For eight paupers
> founded by Bishop John
> AD 1666

Just next to the almshouse is the Pemberton Building.

Pemberton Building

It's a relatively new building being built in 1929.

It is of course used for university lectures, but it is also where the Durham Union Society gathers to debate.

The society began in 1842, long before this building was built, and were a very progressive body. They voted for women to be given the vote, 14 years before it actually happened.

Map 2.4 - Continue to the corner of Palace Green, then turn right to reach the middle of the cathedral.

Durham Cathedral Graveyard

The lawn in front of the cathedral is actually a graveyard, and you can see some very old gravestones sprinkled about.

Map 2.5 - Continue along the front of the graveyard then turn left along the path which will take you to the Cathedral entrance.

As you do, you will see a very tall cross on your right-hand side.

Durham Light Infantry South African War Memorial

You can walk up to it for a closer look.

It is etched with scenes from the Boer war, and the names of the 153 soldiers who died there are to be found around the plinth.

Now make your way to the Cathedral entrance.

The Sanctury Ring

On the door you can see a copy of the famous Sanctury Ring. It is not the original; it is safely inside the Cathedral Museum.

Sanctuary was an ancient religious concept practiced by many religious buildings. In Durham anyone accused of certain crimes could claim sanctuary at the cathedral by grasping this ring.

The Cathedral would take the claimant inside for a maximum of 37 days. After that time, the fugitive would have to go into exile or face his accusers. The right of sanctuary was abolished in the sixteenth century.

A famous example of sanctuary being given is in the Hunchback of Notre Dame. The hunchback Quasimodo rescued

Esmerelda from execution and took her into Notre Dame Cathedral, shouting "Sanctuary".

The Sanctury Ring face is called a Hellmouth, an entrance to Hell through the mouth of a monster. Look closely at the ring handle. It's actually the legs of a man already half in hell, being bitten at either end by a snake.

If you don't plan to visit the cathedral, continue this walk from "Leaving the Cathedral" on Page 69.

Durham Cathedral

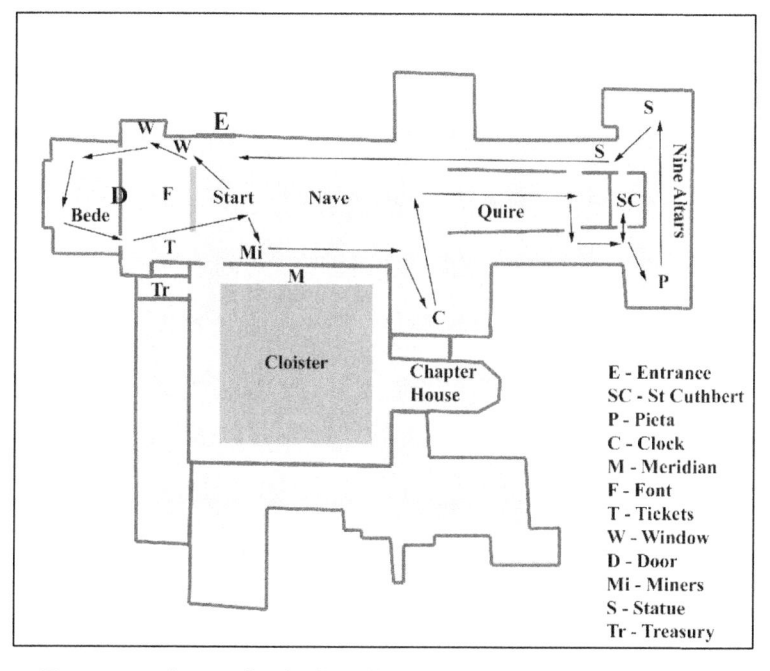

E - Entrance
SC - St Cuthbert
P - Pieta
C - Clock
M - Meridian
F - Font
T - Tickets
W - Window
D - Door
Mi - Miners
S - Statue
Tr - Treasury

Entry to the cathedral will take you through the Galilee Chapel to reach the ticket desk. There you can buy a tour ticket or make a donation and explore the cathedral by yourself.

When you want to continue, make your way to the start of the nave of the cathedral.

The Nave

Look up to the vaulted ceiling.

This type of ceiling, where stone ribs form supportive arches, was an important step in Cathedral architecture. Their use enabled the architects to widen churches and to raise the roof upwards to God. Durham Cathedral is the earliest example of this type of construction.

The Columns

The lines of stone pillars separate the nave from the two side aisles. They are beautifully decorated with spirals, chevrons, and zig-zag patterns. It is said that the spiral columns are symbolic of prayers rising up to God.

Face towards the altar and then turn round to look at the ground behind you.

The Line

Initially women were banned from the cathedral altogether. Why? Because it was believed that St Cuthbert did not want women anywhere near his tomb which sits at the other end of the cathedral.

Since women were not welcome, they started to visit other holy sites, and more importantly they took their donations and gifts with them.

So, the monks of Durham Cathedral eventually compromised by laying this line of stones, beyond which women were not allowed to pass. The black line is made of frosterly marble, which is a limestone embedded with fossils.

Queen Philippa visited Durham with her husband Edward III in the fourteenth century. One evening she visited the cathedral but was stopped from crossing the line by the monks. She brought her husband into the argument and was highly embarrassed when he took the side of the monks.

Later the cathedral added the Lady Chapel behind the Line. It was renamed the Galilee Chapel, and you passed through it coming into the Cathedral.

The Font

Durham's marble baptismal font is totally dwarfed by its oak canopy. It's one of the tallest and most elaborate in England.

The font sits near the entrance to the cathedral, to symbolise the start of a baptised baby's life as a Christian.

Stained Glass

There are also some interesting stained-glass windows at this end of the nave.

Face the nave and turn left. You will see a very modern window.

Daily Bread

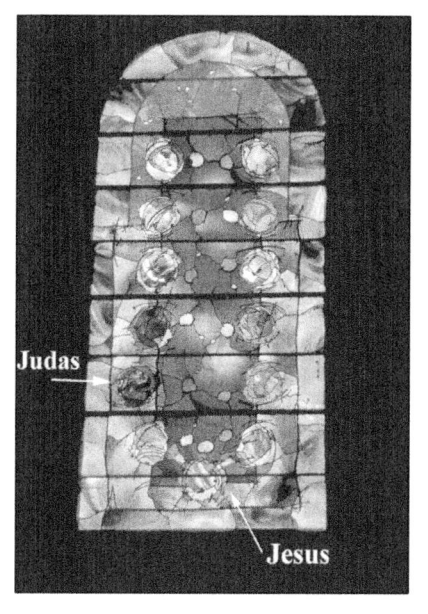

This window is called Daily Bread, but its actually a depiction of the Last Supper. It's probably the most unusual last supper you will see. It shows the head tops of Jesus and his disciples from a high vantage point.

It was given to the cathedral by the local branch of Marks and Spencer.

Take a few steps to the left of Daily Bread to find the RAF Memorial Window.

RAF Memorial Window

It shows a black eagle carrying an airman to paradise to be welcomed by an angel.

At the bottom is Durham City shrouded in mist.

During the Blitz, the Luftwaffe bombed as many significant locations and buildings as they could, and Durham Cathedral would have been an easy target, high on its hill.

In 1942 the air-raid warnings sounded that an attack was imminent. A mist suddenly rose up from the river and covered the city and the cathedral; the Luftwaffe flew past, missing their target.

Look at the floor slabs beneath the window.

Josef Boruwlaski

Spot the one with a simple JB etched on it. That is the burial spot of Josef Boruwlaski who you read about on walk 1.

Turn left and take a look at the window above the door.

St Cuthbert

Turn a little more left to see a window bearing Saint Cuthbert himself. He is of course behind the line, but perhaps women don't annoy him anymore.

Make your way to the Galilee Chapel via the door beneath St Cuthbert.

Galilee Chapel

This chapel was added to the cathedral forty years after the cathedral's construction. You can see just by looking at the columns that building techniques had improved, as the columns are much slimmer and topped with intricate arches.

Look above the arches to see what's left of the colourful paintings which would once have filled this chapel.

You can just about make out the figures of four saints, all in the process of dying horribly and achieving sainthood. The one on the right is Saint Peter who was crucified upside down.

Make your way to the centre of the Galilee Chapel and stand so that there are windows on three sides and a large blocked wooden door on the fourth side.

Great West Door

That is the Great West Door, and in front of the door sits the tomb of Bishop Langley.

He clearly thought he should be the centre of attention; he was very specific about where his tomb was to be placed, regardless of the obstruction it would cause. Since the Great West Door was being blocked, two side doors to the chapel were added.

To the right of the blocked wooden door is the black marble tomb of the Cathedral's second most important resident, the Venerable Bede.

The Venerable Bede

He lived in the eighth century and was the first great historian of England. His writings are responsible for much of what we know about the Middle Ages today. He wrote the Ecclesiastical History of the English People and is known as The Father of English History. He lived, worked, and died in Jarrow which lies further north.

Somehow Durham Cathedral got hold of his remains from Jarrow monastery. No-one knows how really, but the most popular story involves a monk called Alfred who looked after the tomb of St Cuthbert in the eleventh century.

Alfred visited Jarrow monastery and was concerned that The Venerable Bede's bones were not being looked after properly. He decided they should be moved to Durham, which of course would make Durham even more famous and a bigger magnet to pilgrims.

He "took" the bones and scarpered back to Durham. He then put the bones inside the same coffin as Saint Cuthbert. Later the bones were placed in the tomb you see today. On the tomb is inscribed:

HIC SUNT IN FOSSA BEDAE VENERABILIS OSSA

Here are buried the bones of the Venerable Bede

Leave the Galilee Chapel and return to the nave.

Face the altar, then make your way over to the aisle on your right-hand side.

Just beyond the cathedral entrance you will find the Miners Memorial on your right.

Miners Memorial

As mentioned earlier, the miners played a huge role in Durham's society. This memorial was placed in the cathedral in 1947 and as it declares it commemorates:

> The Durham Miners who have
> given their lives in the pits
> of this county, and those who
> work in darkness and danger
> in those pits today.

You can see the Book of Remembrance beside it, and inside are the names of boys and men who died in the pits over the years. Poignantly, it is illuminated by a miner's lamp.

Continue down the right-hand aisle.

As you do you will see splashes of colour on the walls, reminding us that once this cathedral was a riot of colour. It's only now that we expect the rather drab grey stone of cathedrals.

Pause when you reach the transept and look right to see the cathedral's magnificent clock.

The Astronomical Clock

It's estimated that 3,000 Scottish soldiers fought for King Charles II during the English Civil War and were defeated by Cromwell's army at the Battle of Dunbar. They were imprisoned here in the cathedral.

Recently two mass graves have been found in the Cathedral grounds and it's believed they are the Scottish soldiers who did not survive that imprisonment. It's thought that about 1700 died and more mass graves are probably still waiting to be discovered.

The cathedral was bitterly cold to live in and many died of cold and starvation. The prisoners burned almost all the wood in the cathedral in an attempt to keep warm, but it's said that they spared this wooden clock because it is decorated with a thistle, the symbol of Scotland. You can see the thistle at the top of the clock.

Below the thistle are three astronomical dials. Below those you can see the clock face itself. It originally only had one hand, and if you look closely at the clock face, you will see that there are four small divisions between the hours rather than five.

Those four divisions are for the quarter hours, rather than individual minutes in modern clocks. So, the single hand of this clock would point explicitly to 2:15 for example, by pointing to the first division after 2. The clock has of course been updated these days to have the standard two hands.

A secret door

Below the clock you will see two doors decorated to look like the interior of a cathedral.

The doors lead to a small chamber which is not open to the public. However when a service is on, the choir wait in that chamber. At the appropriate time, they exit by these doors and make their way to the quire which you will see shortly.

With the clock behind you, walk to the middle of the transept to stand with the central tower above you.

Central Tower

If you have the energy and time, you can climb the tower for great views over County Durham.

The tower has had a few rebuilds over the centuries, and today stands at 66 metres high. It has ten bells, the heaviest weighing in at 1400 kg.

There is a nice tale which tells us that the monks climbed up the tower to watch the battle of Neville's Cross which took place not far away. When the monks saw the Scots being defeated, they started to sing. For many years, the monks marked the anniversary of that victory by once again climbing the tower and singing.

From where you are standing you can see the nave on one side, and the ornate quire and equally ornate screen on the other side.

Gilbert Scott Screen

The quire screen was installed in the late nineteenth century. The black columns holding it up are made of Frosterley marble, the same stone as the "do-not-pass line" inflicted on the ladies of the congregation all those centuries earlier.

Look up to the central arch to see a cross. It is called a pectoral cross and is a copy of the cross found inside Saint Cuthbert's coffin. If you visit the cathedral museum, you will see it.

Above the pectoral cross is a Celtic cross, commemorating Aidan of Lindisfarne. Aidan was an Irish monk, and it was he who started the conversion of northern England to Christianity by building his priory on the isle of Lindisfarne.

Make your way through the quire towards the Great Rose Window.

The Quire

Durham Cathedral has a quire, unlike most cathedrals and churches which call this area the choir.

It has beautifully carved woodwork but as you have probably guessed, it is a replacement for the original woodwork which went towards keeping some of Cromwell's Scottish prisoners alive.

Look up to see the organ pipes on your left-hand side – they are beautifully decorated. You can't actually see most of the pipes, there are 5,746 of them!

The Rose Window

You actually get the best view of the rose window from here in the quire. If you are lucky the sun will be out and shining through the glass, casting a rainbow of colour around you.

It is decorated with Jesus and his apostles in the middle. They are then surrounded by important characters from the bible.

At the end of the quire, face the rose window and turn right.

Bishop Hatfield

There you will see the multi-coloured decoration around the tomb of Bishop Hatfield, and a stairway which leads up to the cathedra – the throne on which the Bishop of Durham sits.

Bishop Hatfield was determined that the cathedral's throne would be the highest in Christendom, so he sent some monks off to Rome with a ruler to measure how high the throne in St Peter's was.

He then had this throne placed two inches higher. The tale goes on to tell us that the Pope was fuming when he heard and took to using a cushion to sit above Durham's Bishop.

Look just below the stairway to spot the head of Edward III just next to his coat of arms. Bishop Hatfield was a friend of the king, so he was permitted to add this depiction of the king to his tomb.

A Friend Indeed

The friendship between the King and Bishop Hatfield was made clear when Bishop Hatfield entered an argument with the Archbishop of York.

The Archbishop claimed seniority and the right to turn up at Durham cathedral whenever he felt like it. Bishop Hatfield retorted that the Archbishop would have to request an invitation.

The King had to mediate and decided that the Archbishop of York would indeed have to request an invite to Durham.

Now turn towards the high altar to admire the Neville Screen behind it.

Neville Screen

It was paid for mostly by Lord Neville and was carved from stone imported from Normandy, carved in London, and assembled in Durham.

The empty niches in the screen originally held alabaster statues of saints and angels, as well as the Virgin Mary and Saint Cuthbert. When the destruction of the reformation started, the monks of Durham Cathedral hid the statues to save them.

However, the location of their hiding place was forgotten, but most probably involved being buried underground somewhere. They are unlikely to be found now, as the experts tell us that the alabaster would have dissolved long ago.

Leave the quire by either side door and make your way towards the rose window once more. Before you get there, you will reach a few steps leading to a doorway. Make your way up.

St Cuthbert's Shrine

So, after all his wanderings, this is where Saint Cuthbert's remains lie.

Cuthbert's remains nearly didn't survive, as his shrine was dismantled and stripped of treasure by order of King Henry VIII. However, when the coffin was opened to seize any treasure hidden inside, Cuthbert's body was found to still be in its pristine state. This caused a guilty rethink, and the coffin was resealed and reburied.

This of course is not the coffin that Cuthbert was moved around in. You will see that one if you visit the cathedral museum.

Cuthbert and Oswald

Behind the tomb you will see an old statue of Saint Cuthbert carrying a head. It is the head of St Oswald who had been the King of Northumbria and a devout Christian. It was he who gave Lindisfarne to Saint Aidan, leading to the island becoming such a holy place.

He was killed in battle in 642, so his head was transferred to Lindisfarne to be under the care of the monks there. When they fled Lindisfarne with Saint Cuthbert they popped Oswald's head into the coffin for transport, and there it stayed.

Cuthbert's statue lost its own head during the reformation, when decapitating statues of saints was a popular pastime.

Canopy

Look above the tomb to see the colourful canopy. It shows Jesus surrounded by the symbols of the four evangelists who wrote the first four books of the New Testament:

>Matthew: A man
>Mark: A winged lion
>Luke: A winged ox
>John: An eagle

This is a modern cover, a replacement for the original cloth cover which was lost in the reformation.

Facing Cuthbert's tomb, turn left to leave the shrine.

Once you have descended the shrine steps, turn left, and descend a few more steps to reach the Chapel of the Nine Altar. It runs along the back of the cathedral.

Chapel of the Nine Altars

Durham Cathedral, as the custodian of Saint Cuthbert and Bede the Venerable, became a hot spot for pilgrims. Put simply, the church had more visitors than it could handle.

It was decided to expand this end of the cathedral, to house more altars for the faithful to pray at before visiting the saint's chamber.

The builders soon discovered that the ground at this end of the cathedral wasn't as firm as needed, and they had to dig deeper to hit solid rock. That's why this chapel sits lower than the rest of the cathedral.

Once they had a solid foundation, they built this long chapel and filled it with nine altars. Each alter was named after two saints.

Only three altars are still in use today, named after Saints Hild, Aidan and Margaret.

Pieta

As you enter the chapel, you will be greeted by a very modern depiction of The Pieta, where Mary grieves over the body of her murdered son. It's carved from a beech tree and is strangely evocative.

Moving left, the first altar you will see is that of Saint Margaret.

Saint Margaret
Beside it stands a painting of Queen Margaret of Scotland and her son David who became King David She lived in the eleventh century and was Hungarian but married King Malcom of Scotland. She was much loved by the Scottish people and became a saint in the thirteenth century.

In this painting she is depicted near the end of her life and is clearly unwell.

Black Rood
On the front of the altar, you will see a black cross. It is a reference to the Black Rood, a priceless crucifix which contained a piece of the cross Jesus died on. Margaret brought the relic to Scotland from Hungary.

It was stolen by the English more than once, but its final resting place was here in Durham Cathedral. However, during the chaos of the Reformation it disappeared. Perhaps one day it will resurface.

The Scottish Soldiers
On the other side of the altar is a brass plaque inlaid into the paving stones. It commemorates the Scottish soldiers who died while imprisoned in the cathedral after the Battle of Dunbar.

Moving left again you will reach the large Saint Aiden altar.

Saint Aiden
It depicts the animals and nature of Lindisfarne, and symbols of Saint Aiden's life such as his staff.

Finally, you will reach Saint Hild's altar.

Saint Hild
The kneeling cushions in front of the altar identify the three convents which Saint Hild founded, South Shields, Hartlepool, and Whitby.

To the left of St Hild's altar is a large statue

Bishop Van Mildert

This bishop was a supporter of the miners and encouraged their unionisation. He also helped establish Durham University and actually gave the castle and cash to the University. He was definitely one of the good bishops.

Turn left and leave the Chapel of the Nine Altars. Pause when you reach the steps up to Saint Cuthbert's shrine on your left. On your right is a very modern statue.

Lam'a Sabach'thani

It depicts the crucifixion, with Jesus bending backwards in terrible pain and looking up to heaven for salvation.

The title is in Aramaic, the language the experts believe Jesus would have used. It translates as:

> My God, My God, why have you forsaken me

which according to Saint Matthew and Saint Mark were Jesus's last words as he died.

Make your way to the cathedral entrance door.

Once there, cross the cathedral to go through the door directly opposite. It will take you into the cloister.

Turn left to walk about halfway along the north aisle of the cloister.

Find the only window which has the top opening filled in with a small hole punched through it. The window sits about halfway along the aisle.

View of solar hole from outside

The Cloister Meridian Line

At noon on the longest day of the year, the sun streams through the small solar hole and lands on a point on the floor which is marked with "MERI" "DIES".

On the shortest day of the year, it lands on a second marked location on the cloister wall behind the window, also marked with "MERI" "DIES".

On any day, when the sun hits the line running between the two marked points, it is noon Durham Mean Time. DMT is about six minutes ahead of GMT.

You can also see 5, 10, and 15 etched on both marked points, to mark 5, 10, and 15 minutes past noon DMT.

Continue around the cloister to reach the door of the Chapter House.

As you do, look up to see the wonderful stone faces on the bosses staring down at you. You may also see some pipistrelle bats which roost in the cloister.

Chapter House

The monks gathered in this chamber every morning and sat on the stone seat you see running around its edge. The Prior sat on a special stone seat at the far end of the chamber.

One of the monks would read a chapter from "The Rule of St Benedict", so the chamber was eventually given the name The Chapter House.

The attending monks were also allocated their daily tasks by the senior clergy. So, the senior clergy were also known as "The Chapter".

A Cluster of Bishops

It was decided to ban all burials in the cathedral in honour of Saint Cuthbert, and that rule held true until about 1300.

Any bishop who died was instead put under the floor of the Chapter House, including Bishop Flambard who built Framwellgate Bridge which you may have crossed at the start of Walk 1.

They are still there but are mostly safely covered, letting you only see one or two inscribed flagstones.

Chapter House Today

Sadly, this is not the original Chapter House. It was more-or-less demolished and rebuilt in the eighteenth century. It was later restored to its original design in the nineteenth century.

Despite the restoration, for some reason the Chapter House is now populated with a mishmash of tables and chairs, which makes it all look very uncared for.

The chamber is also famous as Professor McGonagall's classroom in the Harry Potter movies. You will find some movie stills on one of the tables.

You may now want to explore the gift shop, the museum, or the little café before leaving the Cathedral.

Leaving the Cathedral

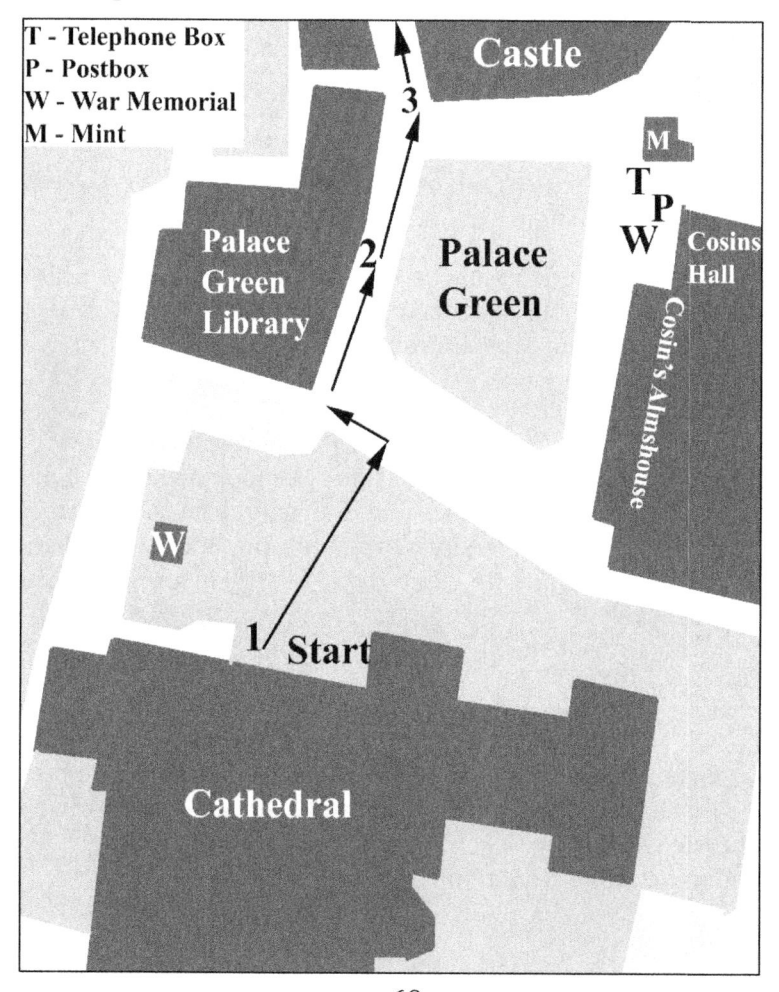

T - Telephone Box
P - Postbox
W - War Memorial
M - Mint

Map 3.1 - Leave the cathedral by the same door you entered and return to the edge of Palace Green.

Turn left and continue walking around Palace Green.

The long group of buildings you reach on your left and which sit directly opposite Cosin's Almshouse is known as the Palace Green Library.

The library actually consists of four buildings which host a vast array of books between them.

The Diocesan Registry

The first one-storey building you reach is relatively new, only built in 1822.

It was the registry of the diocese of Durham where birth, death, and marriage records were stored. It became part of the Palace Green library complex in 1978.

University Library

The next taller building is called the University Library. If you look up, you can see some gargoyles looking back down at you. Apparently, the faces of the gargoyles are those of members of the University at the time the library was being built. It's a shame we can't really see them properly from ground level.

Cosin's Library

Next to University Library is Cosin's Library.

Bishop Cosin had his library built in the seventeenth century. He was a great collector of books and believed in the spread of knowledge. Bibles, Greek and Roman works, philosophy books and other intellectual tombs graced his shelves.

When his library first opened access was strictly limited. Only approved learned men were allowed to see his precious books.

Look above the door to see a bishop's mitre and a Latin inscription. It translates as:

> Not the least part of learning
> is the knowledge of good books

It is beautifully furnished with old wooden book stacks and intriguing ladders to the upper levels. A hidden gem.

So, if you have time try to book a tour. You can do so online at "Cosin's Library Tickets, Multiple Dates | Eventbrite".

Exchequer building

The final building is the Exchequer Building.

It was built in the fifteenth century, and it was where the finances of the Cathedral were dealt with. It also had a court and dungeon to mete out the bishop's justice.

It was built by Bishop Robert Neville, who came from one of the area's most powerful families. It's the Neville coat of arms that you can see between the upper windows. However, the bottom half of the coat of arms has fallen off and the bull at the top has lost his horns.

Map 3.2 - Beyond the Exchequer Building you will find the grand entrance to Durham Castle.

Durham Castle

The castle was built by William the Conqueror, who erected mighty stone castles all over England to keep his newly conquered citizens in check. This one was part of his campaign to "harry the north", which involved murder, starvation, and stripping the local noblemen of titles.

It is the oldest building in Durham, even the Cathedral is twenty years younger.

The castle in Durham was later placed under the control of the Bishops of Durham where it remained for centuries. The castle was then given to the University in 1837 and the students moved in.

Since it is part of the university, the castle can only be visited on a tour. Even if you don't plan to tour the castle, it's worth entering the courtyard by the massive gate. Here you can see how magnificent the castle became under the care of the bishops over the centuries.

The tour will take you to the rooms which are available to the public. Obviously as a working university, quite a lot is off limits.

Exit the Castle

You have now reached the end of this walk.

You have a choice. You might want to tackle Walk 3, or you can return to the lower town as detailed below.

Return to the Lower Town

Turn left to walk along the side of Palace Green – the Cathedral will be on your right-hand side.

When you reach the telephone box, turn left, and descend Owengate.

At the next junction, turn left into Saddler Street which will take you down to Market Place.

Walk 3 - Along the River

This walk starts outside the Cathedral beside the graveyard.

It then takes you down to the riverside where you can enjoy the river and views before returning to Framwellgate Bridge.

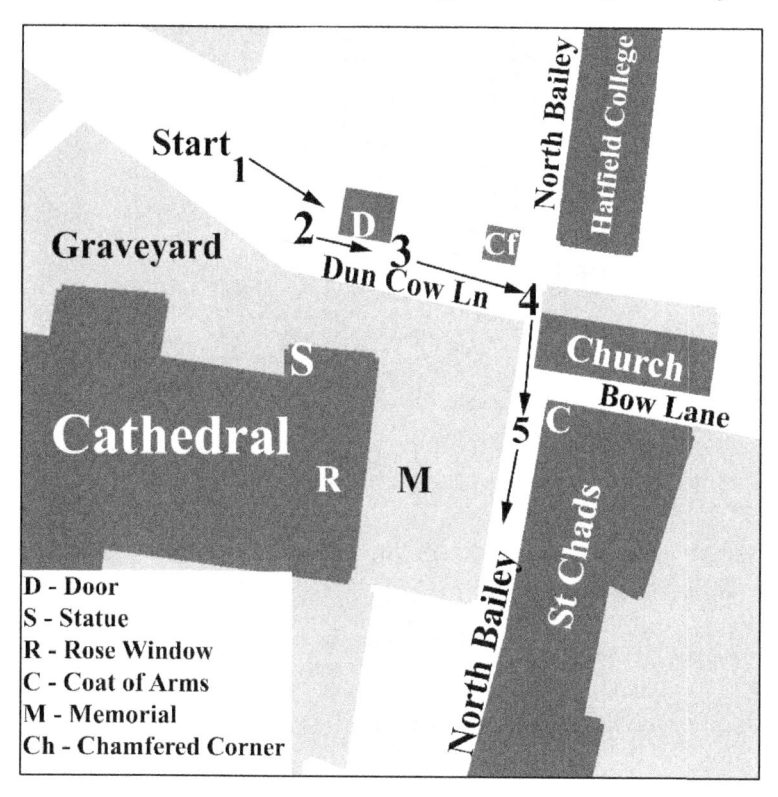

Map 1

Map 1.1 - Facing the cathedral and its graveyard, turn left.

Pause just before you reach Dun Cow Lane, a narrow lane leading downhill.

Look at the cathedral tower on your right. On it you will find the maid and her cow of the Saint Cuthberts legend.

The building in front of you, on the left-hand side of Dun Cow Lane Is called Abbey House.

Abbey House

It was used to house the University's first female students, and was nicknamed the Dovecote, the female students being the "doves"!

Map 1.2 - Make your way down Dow Cow Lane but pause at the old stonework on the side of Abbey House.

Abbey House was built on the site of Lyegate, another of Durham's defenses, which have long disappeared. The old stones you see are thought to be part of Lyegate.

Map 1.3 - Continue to the T-junction with North Bailey.

Protection from Traffic

Take a look at the left-hand corner of Dun Cow Lane.

The ground floor corner has been cut at an angle to avoid the building being scraped and damaged by turning carts etc. It is called a chamfered corner.

The upper floors have a standard right-angled corner, as passing traffic would not have reached that high. The builder has connected the two with decorative stonework.

North Bailey

Most of the buildings along both North and South Bailey belong to, or are used by, one of the University colleges.

College Days

As you explore this area you will doubtless see many students. Each of the colleges has its own College Day when the students and even the staff celebrate their college. So, if you happen to be here on one of those days, you may come across parties and concerts.

Hatfield College

If you look left along North Bailey, you will see the buildings of Hatfield College. It is Durham University's second oldest college and was named after Bishop Hatfield. He was the bishop who ensured that Durham Cathedral's throne was higher than the Pope's.

Map 1.4 - Turn right along North Bailey.

Almost immediately you will see an old church on your left-hand side which was turned into a museum. However, at the time of writing it has been closed.

Bow Lane

The street just beyond the church is cobbled Bow Lane.

It runs down to the riverside and leads to Kingsgate Footbridge. Long ago Kingsgate itself stood at the bottom of Bow Lane, when the river crossing was just a f ord.

Kingsgate

There is a nice legend regarding Kingsgate. William the Conqueror visited Durham in 1072. He was a sceptic regarding the incorruptibility of St Cuthbert's body and send an order that the coffin be opened. He also ordered that if all that was found was a pile of bones, the senior clergy were to be executed.

However, he was immediately struck with a terrible fever, and he was so afraid that it was retribution by the saint that he fled from Durham immediately by Kingsgate and never returned.

Stay on North Bailey and walk past the church and Bow Lane. You will see a line of buildings which face the Cathedral.

St Chads

They form St Chad's college, the third oldest and the smallest college of Durham University. The college members are nicknamed the Chadsians.

The very first building of St Chads, which sits on the corner of Bow Lane and North Bailey, is called Moulsdale Hall and is actually the dining room.

It has a handsome foundation stone from 1961, and above that you can see the coat of arms of Durham.

Map 1.5 - Continue along North Bailey to reach the Cathedral's huge rose window and the WWI Memorial on your right-hand side.

WWI Memorial

The tall column has spirals carved into it, just like the columns in the cathedral itself. Between the spirals are carvings of items from a soldier's kit, including a grenade.

There are no names, just those fateful years:

1914-1918

The building opposite the memorial has "St Chad's College" above the door.

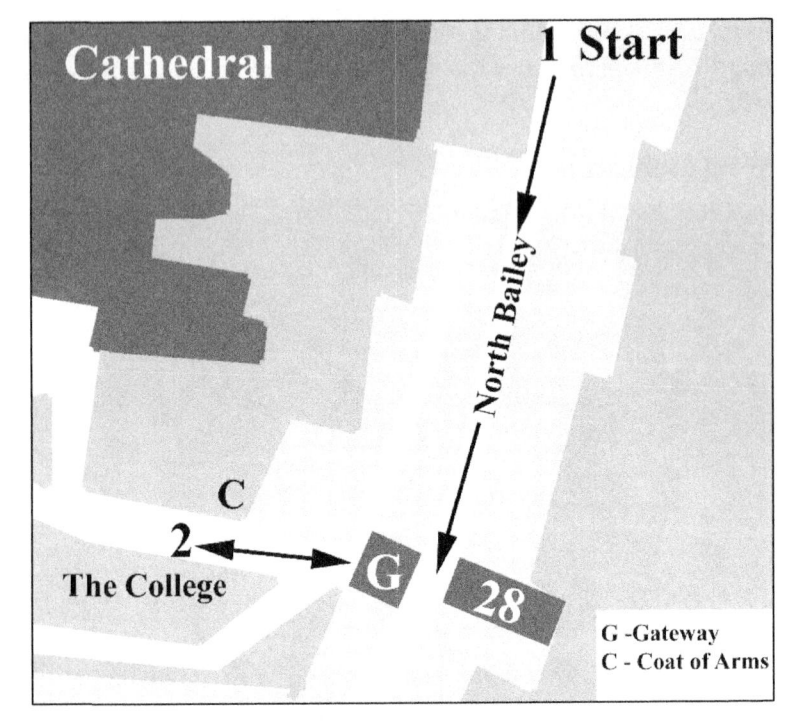

Map 2

Map 2.1 - Continue along North Bailey to reach number 28 on your left-hand side. Opposite it you will see a large gateway.

College Gateway

Look above the archway to spot a chapel window. It was quite common to place a chapel above a monastery gateway. This chapel is dedicated to Saint Helen.

The gateway gives access to an area called The College.

The College

Walk under the gateway and on your left you should find a map of The College and the colourful coats of arms of four bishops which are sprinkled around The College. Some are a lot easier to find than others!

Take a few steps into The College and look above the door of the first building on your right.

You can see the coat of arms of Bishop Egerton, with its bishop's mitre at the top.

The buildings of The College are all converted medieval buildings. They are where the monks lived and worked before Henry VIII closed all the monasteries and kicked the monks out.

The College had an infirmary, a kitchen, and a brewery. Monasteries all over Europe were famous for their ale, but their existence was very practical. Water was often dangerous to drink in medieval times because of disease. Ale was much safer because the brewing process included boiling the water which killed most of the bacteria.

Mao 2.2 – When you have explored The College enough, return through the gateway to North Bailey.

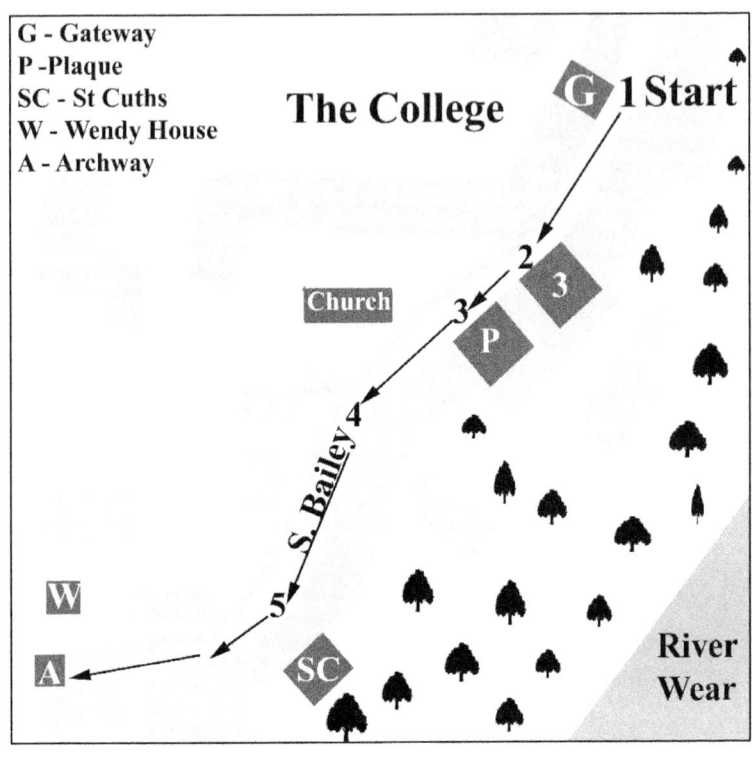

```
G - Gateway
P - Plaque
SC - St Cuths
W - Wendy House
A - Archway
```

The College

Map 3

Map 3.1 - With the College Gateway behind you, turn right to continue along North Bailey.

Just a few steps will take you from North Bailey into South Bailey.

This is one of the most peaceful streets to walk along in old Durham.

Walk along South Bailey to reach Haughton Hall at number 3 on your left. It sits slightly back from the road and is up a little flight of steps.

Haughton Hall

This is home to another of the University's colleges, Saint Johns. You can see the college coat of arms above the door.

It began in 1909 as a theological college, but by 1958 it was offering degrees in many subjects.

Map 3.2 - Make your way a little further down South Bailey to find Bowes House. It has a blue plaque next to the door.

Bowes House

This house has two claims to fame.

A Royal Link
First it was the home of Dame Elizabeth Bowes, an ancestor of Elizabeth Bowes Lyon, the Queen Mother. The Bowes family inherited the Gibside estate in the eighteenth century, and it held some of the richest coal seems in the country. Mining brought great wealth to the Bowes family.

The plaque which commemorates his ancestor, was unveiled by Prince Charles in 2018.

A Literary Link
Bowes House was also once owned by the great-great grandmother of Alice Liddell. Lewis Carrol wrote Alice in Wonderland for little Alice Liddell's entertainment.

Map 3.3 - A little further along you will find St Mary the Less on your right.

St Mary the Less
This old church was founded in the twelfth century, specifically for the soldiers stationed along the city walls. It's now the chapel of St John's college.

Its peculiar name is to distinguish it from the cathedral which is also named after Mary.

Map 3.4 - Continue along South Bailey which now takes you downhill and bends to the right.

Once round the bend, you will see an archway ahead of you. Before you reach it, you will find a walled garden on your right and a building with an ornate doorway on your left.

St Cuthberts Society

The ornate doorway belongs to another of the university's colleges, nicknamed St Cuths.

The walled garden opposite is also part of St Cuthberts. In it stands The Wendy House which provides accommodation for first-year students. It's thought to be called the Wendy House because of the street's link to Lewis Caroll mentioned earlier.

Map 3.5 - Continue towards the archway which is called the Water Gate.

Water Gate

The Water Gate was originally of course one of the defensive gates in the city wall.

It was kept closed at night until the late eighteenth century. At that time, the road was widened to allow carriages to use it, and the gateway was replaced by the archway you see now.

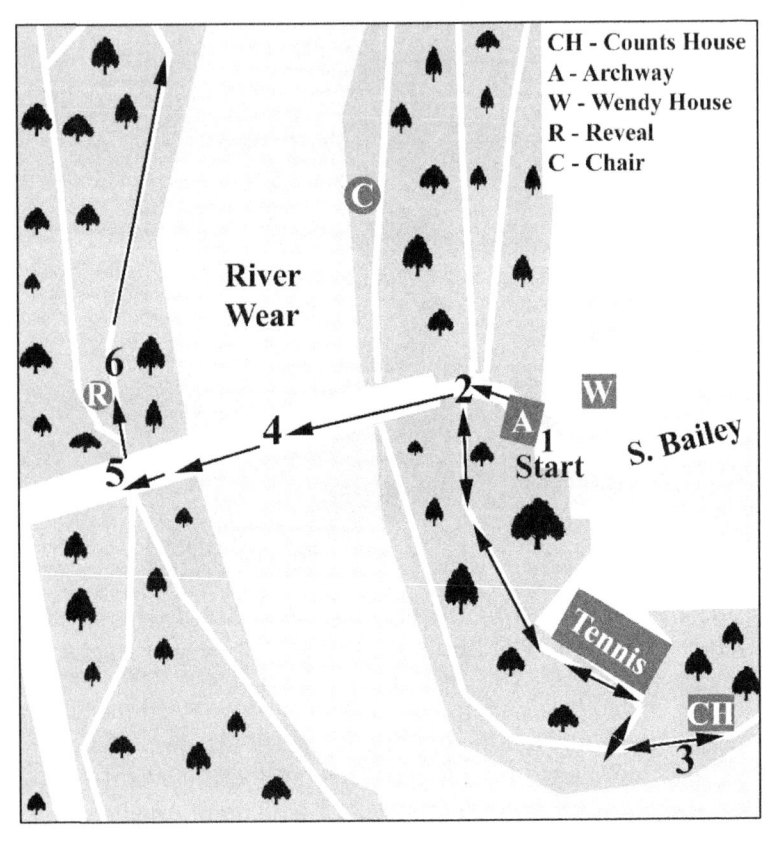

CH - Counts House
A - Archway
W - Wendy House
R - Reveal
C - Chair

Map 4

Map 4.1 - Walk through the archway and follow the path which will descend and bend to the right.

Map 4.2 -Ignore the path which leads off to the right and runs below the city wall. A few more steps and you will see another path on your left.

Take that left-hand path and follow it down to the riverside, where you will find The Count's House.

The Count's House

This pretty little Greek-style folly was built in the early nineteenth century by the then Dean of the Cathedral.

It was named "The Count's House" after Josef Boruwlaski who you read about earlier. However, Boruwlaski didn't ever live in this little house, but he did live nearby.

However, some people did live in it in the early twentieth century. It was even turned into a teashop at one point, serving scones and tea to the tourists who liked to stroll along the riverside.

Map 4.3 - Make your way back up to the main path.

As you do, you will pass a fenced off tennis court on your right. It belongs to St Cuthberts Society and is where Banks Cottage once stood. Banks Cottage was the home of Josef Boruwlaski.

When you reach the main path again, turn left to reach Prebends Bridge.

Prebends Bridge

Prebends bridge gave a private route across the river and through Water Gate. It was originally used only by the Dean and The Chapter of the Cathedral.

The original bridge was lost in the Great Flood of 1771, and this was its replacement.

Make your way to one of the viewing ledges on the bridge and look towards the cathedral.

From here you get great views of the river, the cathedral, and the weir. In summer you will often see boating crews practicing in this stretch of the River Wear.

The artist JMW Turner stood on this bridge to paint the view of the river, cathedral, and the castle. However, he rotated the cathedral more towards the bridge he was standing on, to get a more interesting view.

The painting currently belongs to the National Gallery of Scotland.

On the right-hand bank you can spot Kathedra, a carved stone throne.

Kathedra

It was created in 1988 and is much loved by the locals who have given it many names, including the Gargoyle Chair, the Storytellers Chair, and others. You will often see people sitting on it and taking photographs.

Its real title is Kathedra, which is a play on cathedra, the name of the throne you will find in a cathedral and which the residing bishop sits on.

It looks quite plain from this side, but if you were to look at the back of the throne you would find a mass of carved gargoyles.

Map 4.4 - Make your way over the bridge.

As you near the end of the bridge, spot the etched quotation on the right-hand side of the bridge.

Sir Walter Scott

He was a guest of the bishop at a dinner given in honour of the Duke of Wellington. The inscription is taken from his poem "Harold the Dauntless" which is set in the Durham area.

It reads

> Grey towers of Durham
> Yet well I love thy mixed and massive piles
> Half Church of God, half castle 'gainst the Scot
> And long to roam these venerable aisles
> With records stored of deeds long since forgot.

Map 4.5 - At the end of the bridge you will see paths leading left and right. Ignore those for the moment and stay on the road which climbs to a corner.

At the corner you will see Prebends Cottage.

Prebends Cottage

This lovely little cottage used to be called White Gates Cottage and is thought to have been a tollhouse for Prebends Bridge.

It's one of the most photographed spots in Durham.

Map 4.6 - Return downhill and turn left along the path nearest the bridge. You will soon reach an odd pyramid-shaped sculpture called Reveal.

Reveal

One of Durham Cathedral's towers needed some serious restoration, and Reveal was constructed in 1997 from the sandstone blocks which were removed.

If you look through the opening in the middle of Reveal, you will of course see the cathedral.

Map 4.7 - Continue along the riverside. The path will take you towards the weir and round the back of some buildings which are used as a boathouse.

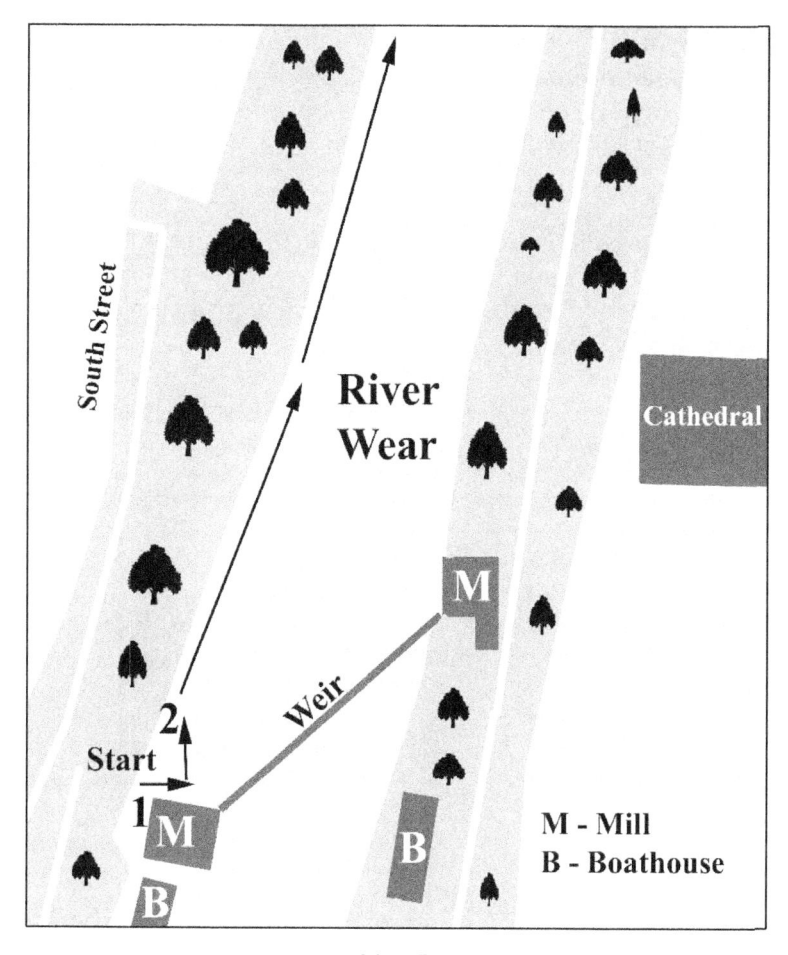

Map 5

Map 5.1 - When you see the river again, you will find a viewing terrace beside an old mill building.

Corn Mill

There were a number of mills on the river, financed and maintained by the cathedral. This one was an old corn mill which used the power of the weir to grind the corn.

Fulling Mill

Let your eye follow the line of the weir and you will see another picturesque old building on the other side of the river. It's another mill which is now owned by the University and is a museum.

It was the Old Fulling Mill where textiles were first cleaned then teased and pounded to produce a thicker warmer product. The weir channelled the water to the mill to provide a source of power for its machinery.

Map 5.2 -Continue along the riverside and enjoy the river and the views of both the cathedral and the castle.

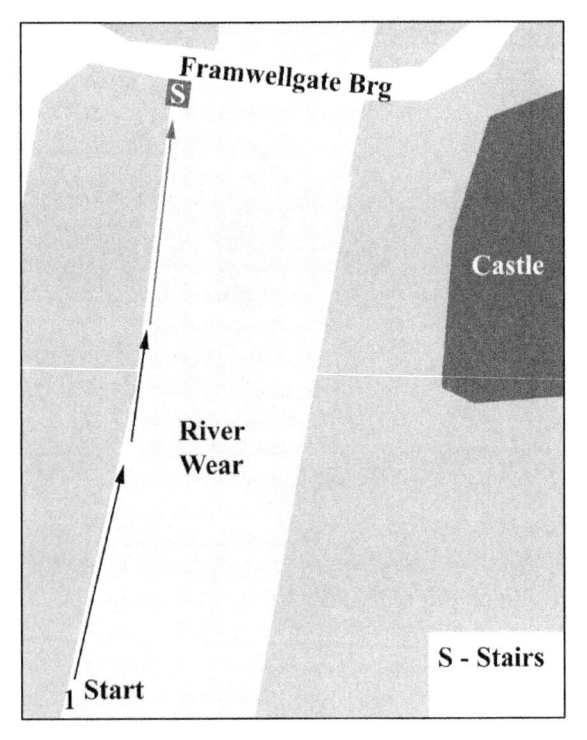

Map 6

Map 6.1 - You will reach a flight of stairs which will take you up to Framwellgate Bridge.

You have now reached the end of this walk.

If you want to get back to Market Place, turn right to cross the bridge and follow Silver Street up the hill.

Did you Enjoy these Walks?

I do hope you found these walks both fun and interesting, and I would love feedback. If you have any comments, either good or bad, please review this book.

You could also drop me a line on my amazon web page.

Other Strolling Around Books to Try

Strolling Around Amsterdam
Strolling Around Arles
Strolling Around Antwerp
Strolling Around Bath
Strolling Around Berlin
Strolling Around Bilbao
Strolling Around Bruges
Strolling Around Delft
Strolling Around Florence
Strolling Around Ghent
Strolling Around Jerez
Strolling Around Lisbon
Strolling Around Ljubljana
Strolling Around Lucca
Strolling Around Madrid
Strolling Around Palma
Strolling Around Pisa
Strolling Around Porto
Strolling Around Rouen
Strolling Around Reims
Strolling Around Sienna
Strolling Around Toledo
Strolling Around The Hague
Strolling Around Verona

Index

A

Abbey House 76

B

Boat Trip 29
Bowes House 85

C

Castle 73
Cathedral 45
Clayport Gate 22
College Gateway 82
Corn Mill 95
Cosin's Almshouse 41
Cosin's Hall 40

D

Drury Lane 33
Durham Light Infantry 17, 43

E

Elvet Bridge 27

F

Framwellgate Bridge 9

Fulling Mill 96

G

Guildhall 16

H

Haughton Hall 85
House of Correction 29

K

Kathedra 91

M

Magdalene Steps 27
Market Place 13
Market Tavern 16
Marquess of Londonderry 14
Moatside Lane 10, 30
Moneyer's Garth 39
Mustard 26

N

Neptune 23
North Bailey 77

O

Owengate 35

P

Palace Green................................ 36
Palace Green Library
   Cosin's Library 70
   Diocesan Registry................... 70
   Exchequer building 72
   University LIbrary................... 70
Pemberton Building 42
Prebends Bridge 90

R

Reveal 94

S

Saddler Street 24

T

Sanctury Ring 44
Silver Street 10
Sir John Duck 11
Sir Walter Scott 91
St Chads 79
St Cuthberts Society 87
St Mary the Less 86
St Nicholas Church 19

T

Teapot 26
The Count's House 89
The North Gate 33
The Shakespeare 30
Timeline 21
Tin of Sardines 28
Town Hall 18

W

Water Gate 88
WWI Memorial............................ 81

Printed in Great Britain
by Amazon